SEVEN STEPS TO START

BILL WOOLSEY

SEVEN STEPS TO START

A Sacramental Entrepreneur's Guide
to Launching Startups that Thrive

Seven Steps to Start

A Sacramental Entrepreneur's Guide
to Launching Startups that Thrive

Printed in the United States of America

First Printing, 2016

ISBN-13: 978-0692692943 (FiveTwo)
ISBN-10: 0692692940

Additional copies may be purchased by contacting:
FiveTwo
PO Box 6526
Katy, TX 77491

fivetwo.com

ACKNOWLEDGMENTS

So many people have poured into me over the years, enabling me to grow in this apostolic, entrepreneurial realm.
A number stand out:

- *Bob Kolb,* the perfect mix of theologian and living.
- *Wray Offermann*, the best senior pastor. Ever.
- *Randy Rutledge*, great friend and great leader.
- *Mark Junkans*, urban and ethnic apostolic guru.
- *Jonathan Reitz,* the Coach of all coaches who pulls out the best and redeems the rest.
- *Timothy*, *Abigail*, and *Samuel*, you are my pride and joy.
- *Julie*, your faith in Jesus and in me make everyday beautiful. I love you.

A special thank you to *RJ Grunewald* for editing this work. You make editing seem easy.

DEDICATION

*To all the men and women who risk starting new
so that more people know Jesus.*

CONTENTS

INTRODUCTION

Holy discontent creates incredible fires.

It kindled two of the ministries I lead: CrossPoint Community Church and FiveTwo Network.

CrossPoint birthed out of a frustration that most of the mainline churches in my denomination spoke a language long gone. While the US went informal in its conversation and writing, my church body stayed formal in speech and action, ignoring the change in the culture and in essence erected a holiness wall that kept Jesus' lost people from the things of Jesus. My desire in starting CrossPoint was to create a congregation that not only spoke the language of the local lost person but also loved that person so much we could not help but speak their language and love their music and adopt as many of their values as possible.

All so that we could introduce them to Jesus.

In the summer of 1996, I took that desire to the Texas District of my denomination, the Lutheran Church - Missouri Synod. Having come from a setting where we spent as much time fending off attacks from the Jesus side of Hell's gates as actually attacking Hell's gates, I knew that with the support of the district leaders the new ministry would flourish like a tree planted by a stream of water.

I asked the president of the district for three things: permission for the congregation to worship in a way that spoke to the lost people of west Houston, support for starting large with multiple-staff from the beginning, and financial support for land and facility.

"Holy discontent creates incredible fires."

The district president responded, "How you worship is a congregational issue, you can have as many staff as you want if you figure out how to pay for them, and how much land are you thinking?"

I asked back, "How much land are you thinking?"
He answered, "10 acres?"
I countered, "40."
"Well, we'll see," he thought out loud.

By the grace of God, the seven families joining us in the start already had a vision for the style of worship the community needed. God led us to a wonderful worship leader and an Energizer administrative assistant, and 46 acres came on the market in the area we wanted to be at an unbelievable price: $.56/square foot, due to the fact that half of the property was in the 100 year floodplain.

As we started construction the Civil Corp of engineers resurveyed the property and decided none of it was in the floodplain any longer. This act of God blessed us financially over the next decade, allowing us to sell 17 acres that paid off the majority of the land and facility debt. God's sovereignty reigned again.

The largest financial blessing, however, arrived in the form of a district and its Church Extension Fund who believed in what we were doing to the extent they backed us financially by not only loaning $3MM to this startup congregation of 100 worshipers, but also by paying the interest on an additional $1.6MM line of credit.

I felt a little like Esther; it seemed that He had created me for a time such as this, entrusting me with experience and location and favor that not everyone receives. Since then, I have worked hard to steward that trust so that more and more people might come to be included in His Family.

That stewarding met a similar discontent and formed FiveTwo.

In 1998, the mission executive in Texas gathered some of us Texas church planters for a time of prayer and encouragement. It so struck me, this one in authority over me actually caring for me, that I was determined to replicate it for other planters around the country. With the generous funding of a mission group out of California, I took the Texas model and added a large dose of fun. For the next eight years, a group of 20+ planters gathered annually, growing in camaraderie and courage on retreats in Phoenix, Arkansas, and Texas.

Throughout those years it became obvious my situation was foreign: most planters were asked to start new wineskin ministries with little support or know-how. No one in their immediate system had a clue about how difficult the task was, nor how to support a planter who was trying to create a new culture in an old system. Many of them were in districts who spoke of reaching the lost but lacked the courage to protect the new ministry and planter, especially when the ministry sought to break out of the old wineskin.

In March 2009, after a few years of grousing about it, I invited 12 church planters to Katy to see what God might bring from our common discontent. We knew well the loneliness of planting, coupled with the lack of experience and mentoring.

We didn't know where we were going so we brought in Will Mancini to guide our 24 hour journey. We wanted to do, not just talk. To act, not just dream.

After 24 hours of praying and debating and cigar smoking (not the entire time), we arrived at FiveTwo. Actually, the name careened out from the doctored brain of Scott Rische who deftly explained the community impact of the feeding of the five thousand, that everything the planter needs to feed his community is already in the community. It just needs to be brought to Jesus for blessing.

We all sat in silent awe.

Silence led to lightbulbs and a quick pregnancy happened: we would launch a church planting network specializing in the "personal how." When it came to planting churches— immigrant, suburban, high cost, low cost, more traditional, crazily progressive—this crew knew how.

And we were sticklers for personal. To a man, we had all been encouraged, inspired and coached by someone. We each had a guy we could pick up the phone and call when we were disappointed or confused.

Great consensus broke out, and we white-boarded the steps to launch a network that brought "personal" and "how" together for those front-line harvesters in the US and around the world. Our goal? Grow FiveTwo from our little group to a local presence in all 29 metro areas in the US, helping lead our denomination's goal of 2000 new starts by 2017. Five years later, in 2014, we have 40 FiveTwo Locals in 37 cities in the US, with requests to bring it to four other countries.

We realized in year two, however, that while we were planters, most people were not. Too many churches tuned out our message. Before we could see large numbers of new congregations in the US, we would need to help congregations learn to start, to embrace their communities and learn new ways of talking and engaging. To take baby steps before they birthed the baby of an entirely new congregation.

We threw open the tent and invited leaders from a variety of stages and a variety of sacramental denominations to join us in learning how to marry our sacramental passion and missional fervor and reach our local communities with the Gospel of Jesus. To not only love the lost people overseas but especially reach the lost people next door.

TIME TO START NEW

We believe that the church must start new to reach new.

The mainline, historical, sacramental church — a small slice of which I belong — has been stumbling to the bottom since the 1960s. As I pen this book, my denomination has not experienced net numerical growth in membership for over 50 years.

This lack of effectiveness in reaching Jesus' lost people in the US, coupled with a fear of the culture in which the Church now finds itself, has produced a discouraging effect. Rather than propel us into more purposeful and creative ways of engaging those who do not know Jesus, we have lost our apostolic, entrepreneurial will. We are afraid to risk, afraid to fail. We have become so focused on doing doctrine right that we shirk doing new.

"We believe that the church must start new to reach new. "

Thus this book on starting well. A book that will help us understand why we should start new and practically how to start new.

Throughout the book you will encounter a two-word term infrequently found together: *sacramental entrepreneur.*

Let me explain the phrase by breaking them apart and then reuniting them like two long-lost lovers, for I believe the historical, sacramental church must realize the strength they provide when united as one.

Sacramental churches are churches that embrace a sacred view of Baptism and the Lord's Supper. In my denomination's lexicon, sacramental applies specifically to these two sacraments. They are sacraments because they deliver Jesus' forgiveness through physical means at Jesus' instigation. They are the vehicle that delivers God's forgiveness. They do not replace the work of Jesus; they amplify it. They are physical and mysterious all at the same time; the promises of God played out in our physical reality.

When I use sacramental I certainly mean the traditional understanding of the sacraments. A sacramental person embraces these mysterious rituals as a grace experience. He will include them in worship experiences because to neglect such life-giving celebrations would be derelict. Sacramental churches are those who hold these views as well, opting for the mysterious, divine working of God rather than simply man moving through some faith motions.

But sacramental expands beyond worship, beyond water, and beyond bread and wine.

The word also describes our existence as the Church. You and I who follow Jesus are sacramental. The presence of Christ lives in us. Collectively we are His Body; individually we are His ambassadors. We emit His odor--a decay of death to those who deny him but a fragrance of life for those who trust His claims.

We are the means through whom God desires to bless our neighbors.

The single mom might not experience His grace if I didn't mow her lawn. My sales manager might think God merely a demanding deity had I not invited him to dinner with my family. While the real presence of Jesus is offered us in food elements in worship, the real presence of Jesus is also offered to my neighbor in real people elements every day: in the baptized body of believers known as The Church.

A sacramental entrepreneur is a Christ-follower who desires to start new in order to connect new people to Jesus and His Church. The title applies to church planters, small business owners, young college graduates, and even stay-at-home moms. Start new to bring the presence of Jesus to new people.

If you believe the Spirit of Jesus is at work in you, seeking to bring Jesus to your world, and you desire to start a new creation that helps others discover this life-giving truth, then this book is for you.

The following flows from decades of conversations and contemplations about starting. Whether on a corporate level — small groups, youth servant events, new ways of preaching, and new congregations — or individual — perennial flower gardening, losing 30 lbs, or learning how to swim at the age of 53 — I discovered that regardless of the start, each start had common ingredients that unfolded in a similar order; seven key steps that I now consciously follow.

My goal is very simple: to help you to start sacramental communities that connect people with Jesus and usher those people into His baptized body of believers on earth. If sacramental speaks to the mysterious working of God through tangible means, then be God's sacrament in your communities so that people encounter the presence of Jesus.

PRESENCE BEFORE STARTING

"To think that you must abandon conversation with God in order to deal with the world is erroneous."
-- Brother Lawrence

If you read the table of contents, you might have noted the absence of prayer. For a book about starting sacramental communities that connect people to Jesus, one would think prayer an essential ingredient. And you would be correct.

Rather than include prayer in a step, however, I want to discuss it as presence.

Prayer as presence entails living life certain that Christ is really present in you and certain His ear continually turns your way. Prayer flows from a divine relationship gifted to you from your Creator, through His Son, and indwelled by His Spirit.

Prayer belongs before you begin and after you end, sometimes loud, other times soft, but never silent.

The work you are attempting, bringing the Kingdom of Heaven into Satan's realm, rescuing Jesus' people from Satan's grip, is a sacramental work. Jesus is doing his work in the world in, with, and through you. Prayer isn't a one-time exercise to be checked off the list, but an ongoing purposeful conversation with the One who will decide whether or not your desire becomes a reality.

Before you start, embrace the presence of Christ in you as a reminder of the need for constant, conversational prayer.

SPEAK YOUR HEART

"Delight yourself in the LORD,
and he will give you the desires of your heart."
Psalm 37:4 (ESV)

Inherent in this verse lies the chicken or the egg question, "Which comes first?" The Psalmist describes an if/then clause: if you delight in the Lord, then he will give you the desires of your heart. Undoubtedly this is a developmental verse for your heart: As I seek joy by doing God's will, my heart grows to love the delights of its creator.

Allow this verse to move beyond your heart to also develop your prayer life. Speak to Jesus about your deep desires like you would to a dear friend. And pray that the delights of your Creator would also become your delights.

One core delight of our Creator is "...not wishing that any should perish, but that all should reach repentance." (2 Peter 3:9 ESV). If that is your heart's desire, then pray through your plan and desire to keep people from perishing. And if it is not your heart's desire, pray that God would give you a heart that desires "...to seek and to save the lost" (Luke 19:10 ESV). Pray for your start. Pray for the desires of your heart as the sacramental entrepreneur. Pray for the people you want God to send. Even spend time focusing on the details in your prayers; pray for specific numbers, names, and even particular times of the day.

Keep these desires in your conversations with your Creator constantly, starting immediately.

STEP 1
KNOW YOUR PASSION

"The true soldier fights not because he hates what is in front of him, but because he loves what is behind him."
--G.K. Chesterton

I recently visited with a new church planter. His was the complete outfit: slightly ripped jeans, plaid shirt, and cool, thick-framed glasses. The GQ of church planters.

When I asked him why he was starting his church, his answers spoke of great logical and spiritual truths. People were going to hell without Jesus and local churches were out of touch with the unchurched in the community. But while the answers rang true, they failed to reveal why he was starting a church. What inside of him was driving him to make this sacrifice, to redirect his family, and take such a risk?

His wrappings looked sharp but I longed to hear his heart.

I was waiting to hear a story.

I wanted a compelling call that pulled me in. I wanted the story of a co-worker who came to faith because of a slow-building relationship. The testimony of a father, on his death bed, rejecting Jesus with his final breath. I wanted to hear about the divine discontent with the congregational status quo that gave voice to his childhood experience. What was the story behind the story that compelled him to move to a new community and pursue bi-vocational ministry?

YOUR WHY

The first step in starting new is to grasp the "why." Why start new? Why open a new coffee shop? Why start the leadership development class for teens? Why learn to swim? Why plant a church or begin the preschool?

'Why?' is a values question.

Values and passion are closely related; when you see one you are given a glimpse of the other. When people become passionate, they reveal their values. If you want to know your values, find out what makes you excited or angry.

The 'why' flows from passion. The why is a part of how you've been wired. It's a part of the way God has formed your community.

THE 'WHY' BEHIND APPLE

In the book Start With Why, Simon Sinek describes the values of Apple, Inc. At first thought, you might think that the 'why' of Apple is to make great, beautiful, user-friendly computers. But that's not the 'why' that flows deep within Apple.

Simon Sinek describes what Apple's 'why' actually looks like:

Everything we do, we believe in challenging the status quo. We believe in thinking differently. The way we challenge the status quo is by making our products beautifully designed, simple to use and user-friendly. And we happen to make great computers.

Wanna buy one?

The 'why' actually has nothing to do with what they do. And yet it has everything to do with what they do. The products, the design, the retail stores, the pricing structures, and the innovation might all be important, but they are not the 'why.'

The 'why' is what makes Apple different.

COMMON PASSION

As sacramental entrepreneurs, we share a passion for Jesus and His sacramental presence. He wraps His divine mystery in our physical mundane bodies. The business you start, non-profit you launch, the church you plant, or leadership classes you offer provide opportunities for people to experience Jesus through you. God is at work in very mysterious, yet ordinary ways as we do our work.

This common passion drives everything we do.

As sacramental entrepreneurs, Jesus resides at the center of 'why,' His love, His work, and His glory compel us to action.

Often when asked "Why?", we fail to go deep to the passion-source. We answer in terms of head instead of heart, logically instead of emotionally, corporately instead of personally. We deal in facts instead of stories.

But passion has a story.

"Passion has a story."

Tell me about your internal struggle. Paint me a picture of the phoenix rising from the ashes that led you to form the non-profit where you took out loans on your credit cards because you believed in something so deeply. Connect the dots so that I see the why behind your life-changing journey.

Tell me your story. Show me your heart so that I understand your sacrifice and so that I want to sacrifice. Tell me your passion, not just our common passion but your unique passion.

GROWING GROUPS OF PEOPLE

I discovered my passion in about year seven of public ministry. Through a course called Network that interwove passion, spiritual gifts, and personal style, I discovered the passion that drove me and vision that drew me in. For the first time I realized my passion was to "grow groups of Christians, the larger the better."

I love to watch people gather around a cause and be transformed by a calling. I live for seeing the light bulb turn on in the head previously living in darkness. And one now-lit head is not enough for me, I want to see lots of people experience that. The more the merrier.

This passion existed in me before the discovery, but since then it purposefully informs everything I do. My passion is to reach God's lost people now; to change what needs to be changed and risk what needs risking now.

And to do that in ways that reach lots of lost people.[1]

THE INNER YOU

While passion may generate negative images, and certainly can be used for evil, I use the term to speak of the driving desires and unique wiring the Creator embedded in you. These are the gifts spoken of in the First Article of the Apostles' Creed when we confess, "I believe in God the Father Almighty, Creator of heaven and earth."

They are what Luther speaks of when he says, "God has made me and all creatures; that He has given me my body and soul, eyes, ears, and all my members, my reason and all my senses…"

It's the me spoken of in Psalm 139 when it says, "You knit me together in my mother's womb."

Your First Article realities speak to why you love swimming, gravitate to racing, and salivate when steaks sear on the grill. Your First Article realities entail your abilities to compute numbers quickly, understand languages easily and pilot a boat with confidence regardless of the size.

Passions flow from your natural, God-given abilities. God placed them in you so that those loves would be lived out in the world. When we allow our Christian faith to envelop them, they become a natural driver for reaching people who do not know Jesus.

[1] One of the best tools that helped me discover this was APEST. www.apesttest.com

THE 'WHY' BEHIND SWIM PRACTICE

In the summer of 2014, at the age of 53, I learned how to swim. I vaguely remember a bad swimming experience when I was six. Since then, I could do a modified dog paddle at best. I was afraid to put my face underwater. I hated how water went up my nose and had come to the conclusion something physiologically hindered me from "blowing bubbles" effectively. "I can't do it," was my response. "I must have a deviated septum." I did not even know if a deviated septum could cause such an inability but it sounded official and stopped people from exploring deeper.

In the fall of 2013 I volunteered to lead the Boundary Waters trip for my son's Boy Scout troop. Somehow I failed to read the fine print: since the trek would take us over 30 miles from base camp, on open water, all attendees were required to pass a 100 yard swim test. 75 yards of a strong stroke (free, breast or side), followed by 25 yards of a resting back stroke. I lived in denial until March. When I fully grasped this expectation, I began to come to grips with what I was going to have to do.

For six weeks in May and June, my daughter, then one of the elders at my church, and finally my wife and son all contributed to teaching me how to swim so that I could pass the test. Almost daily I angrily told my wife I did not think I was going to be able to do it. If I failed, the group would not be able to go into Canada since I was one of the required adults. My whole family suffered during that time.

On Sunday, June 15th, Father's Day, I took the test...and passed!

This 53-year-old man can now jump in the water, blow bubbles effectively, and swim the free style, with some side stroke help for 75 yards.

The day I completed the test was one of the most rewarding days of my life.

What drove me to daily practice and overcome my past fears? It was not the beauty of the Canadian Boundary Waters. And it certainly was not the desire to learn how to swim. Learning to swim was a means to an end, but not the end.

My love for my son and desire to experience this once-in-a-lifetime trip with him drove me to learn to swim. I learned not for me; I learned so that I could take the trip with him. He was my passion.

SENSED AND SEEN

Your passion is critical in startups because the heart of the startup takes on the heart of the sacramental entrepreneur. What you value becomes what the group values. People will join your cause because of the culture created by your values.

Your passions produce atmospheric results; it will create a culture that is both sensed and seen. Your gatherings find their breath in your values. People might say, "I love how this feels" or "It has a great vibe."

That sense only lasts a while, however, if not reinforced by what is seen. Values are only true if they are not only sensed, but lived out. A person's experience will verify what they felt; their experience will give them a window to the passion and values of your startup.

Jesus spoke of a similar phenomena in Luke 6:45, "The good person out of the good treasure of his heart produces good, and the evil person out of his evil treasure produces evil, for out of the abundance of the heart his mouth speaks" (ESV) .

Sacramental entrepreneurs grasp the connection between heart and hand, between passion and actions.

"Your passion is critical in startups because the heart of the startup takes on the heart of the sacramental entrepreneur."

IF THIS STEP NEEDS SHARPENING...

Read the book of Acts, a chapter a day for the next month. Make a list of all of the risks taken by the apostles and leaders.

If you are unsure of the passion God has placed in you, try these exercises:

i. If you could snap your fingers and do anything, with no money, failure, family or time limitations, what would you do?

ii. Looking back over your life, where have you seen fruit produced at the greatest level? Where have your gifts been affirmed?

iii. What events or experiences have brought you the most joy and satisfaction?

iv. Gather two or three trusted friends and ask them to describe your particular gifts. "If I could only be used for one or two activities, how would you use me?"

v. What vacations or hobbies have brought great satisfaction? List the ingredients of those times.

After completing the above, gather the responses. What common words did you use? What common themes and threads exist?

Can you state your passion in one sentence beginning with "My heart's desire is to…"

SHARPEN TO START QUESTION

What are you passionate about that could grow into a ministry or business which positions you to share Jesus with people? What love of your heart could earn you the right to speak into someone's life because you are bringing value to their life?

STEP 2
GET PERSPECTIVE

"Everywhere is walking distance if you have the time."
--Steven Wright

In our family, we encourage our children to turn their passion into pay no later than their freshman year of high school. This desire led our oldest son to turn his love for computers into a network administration job at a church at the age of 16. It led our daughter to a massive summer swim lesson business.

When we first thought about our 14-year-old son offering piano lessons, our perspective was, "No one would take lessons from a 14-year-old. They'll want an adult instructor." We believed that he was a talented piano player. We even knew he was the top student in his instructor's studio, but our false belief about what people valued in a piano teacher insisted that he's not old enough. And this almost sabotaged him before he ever started.

Had we allowed that false perspective to remain, we would not have moved forward...and he would not have six students in less than six months, one of whom is much older than he is.

Perspective can change everything and it will play a significant role in your start. It can provide a view of a situation that can suck hope from the soul and slam doors for no reason. Or it can turn pain and questions into gorgeous sunsets and valleys.

At this writing, my daughter has suffered from one, long severe headache for almost a year. Numerous doctors later, they all converged on one non-life-threatening diagnosis. While their collective wisdom did not remove the pain, it did remove the fear of death. This new perspective on her condition ushered her into a new more hopeful hallway, with a defined destination. No more wondering what to do.

Without this new perspective, it would have been a lot more difficult to keep moving forward. But a new perspective changed the way we saw everything.

In our starts, the right perspective changes everything. But this perspective is disproportionately affected by at least four specific realities.

FEARS

"You were supposed to bring 12' pieces of rope, not 8'."

Four feet doesn't seem like much. But when you fear heights like I do, and the cable route up the Half Dome stares you in the face while your two sons, whom you promised your wife you would protect, stand nearby, and eight feet means they cannot tie the three of you off as safely as the others in the trek, four feet means failure.

I contemplated telling my two sons we were not going up, that's how afraid I was.

I knew that would make me a jerk, but at least I would be an alive jerk with two alive sons. Thankfully one of the scouts showed us another knot needing much less rope, and after tugging on the knot for dear life, I let go of some of the angst.

We survived the climb.

In hindsight we laugh at my fear: at least one-third of all the climbers on the route did so without any safety ropes. My youngest son made the descent on the outside of the cables, clipped in only because I threatened him.

The climb revealed fear's grip on my perspective. It sucked much of the joy of the last part of the trek right out of me. All I could see was my body bouncing off the rocks on the way down.

FEAR IS ALSO YOUR FRIEND

Like much of life, fear works both ways. In startup situations, fears become your friend. They often focus you on solutions.

"Rather than belittle your fears, treat them like best friends."

Rather than belittle your fears, treat them like best friends. Turn the tables on them. No need to emasculate them at this stage, leverage them. They will clarify where you need help, either make it obvious where you need to overcome a fear emotionally or bridge a gap intellectually.

If I am afraid we might run out of money prematurely, I probably need to sit down with a money person and talk through different options. I would be stupid to ignore that fear.

If I am afraid the community will not support this new center, I might want to sit down with some key holders and get their thoughts. I would be stupid to ignore that fear.

If I am afraid I will lose the house because my startup might fail, I might want to talk this over with my spouse and see if she is okay with the risk. I would be really, really stupid to ignore that fear.

Fears help us focus on the areas we need to address. They identify where knowledge is missing. They push us to discover ways around or through.

COMMON STARTUP FEARS

- There won't be enough money.
- I won't be able to find the right people.
- It can't be done.
- It's not going to work.
- If this doesn't work, my reputation will be trashed.
- I won't be able to find another job.
- We won't be able to pay the bills.
- My kids will hate me.
- My spouse will never forgive me.
- Others in my field (pastors, business leaders, non-profit leaders) will disown me.

FAITH

Fears and faith intermingle, for sure. But I separate them because they should be. Fear cements your feet to the ground; faith frees your feet to explore. At least it should if you are a sacramental entrepreneur. We believe the Jesus who walked the earth now walks the earth in us. His sacred presence lives wrapped in our physical presence.

That is somewhat liberating, don't you think?

So what do you believe about God?
About the world?
About yourself?

FAITH | GOD & YOU

The God of the Bible knows all about you and all about the world around you. His awareness transcends the ticking of the clock and the thickness of your skin. While your soul appears invisible to me, no nuance passes unseen before Him. He is both judgmental and forgiving, jealous in His knowledge and His love.

His perfection flows into His standards for us: nothing short of perfection satisfies His demands. Nothing short of His perfect Son satisfies His demands of us.

When you are born again into His family, you receive everything the Son Jesus has to offer. God's standards are met. Your sin, forgiven. Jesus' perfection, yours.

This new identity, child of God, and new relationship, friend instead of enemy, sometimes begins and is always cemented in your baptism. You can mark your faith on your calendar. No need to doubt your Jesus status when "Baptism Day" is inked on your page. No need to go hungry when the Lord's Supper is set at the gathering.

Is God mean? If hating evil regardless of where it lives defines God's meanness, then yes, He's mean. Allowing Jesus to take your place in the punishment arena, however, shifts the meanness onto His Son, out of love for you.

You only get love.

Your baptism confirms this love in your life, throughout your life. His Supper solidifies those promises in your heart so that when your feet grow sluggish and your hands, calloused, your trust in His love remains strong.

You trust that his presence is constant, his generosity is bottomless, and his grace flowing freely.

This extreme expression of love trickles into the little crevices of life. It even trickles into our business startups and venture funding. He honors our work done in His name and for the extension of His kingdom.

FAITH | GOD & YOU & THE WORLD

Too often those of us who lead in the Church forget the Church operates in the same system and by the same rules that the world does, except for one: divine forgiveness. The grace of Jesus flows only from the Church, from God's Word through God's people.

Sacramental entrepreneurs operate in this world God created. They bring their new mindset, but they embrace how the world works, knowing their growth in these areas afford them more opportunity to speak Jesus into the world.

Faith in a Creator God leads Sacramental Entrepreneurs to welcome God's scientific design on multi-levels as gifts from His hands. Faith in a God who designed the entire universe, even the world I live in, even the body my soul calls home. This faith provides a new variety of tools available to me in starting well.

God wove multi-faceted beauty throughout His creation in countless ways. Utilize every facet of that beauty every way possible.

Communication strategies, word-of-mouth power, leveraging social media, cash flow, art in the form of music and dance, how to manage children, how to manage staff and volunteers...the list extends for miles. Even apparently disorganized, organic free-flowing movements follow some kind of organizational theory.

Note: I made a list of some of my favorite scriptures on faith if you want to dive into some verses about this area.
http://www.fivetwo.com/verses/

FAILURE

What do you believe about failure?

I believe there are two types: fatal and non-fatal, and two arenas: on earth and beyond my time on earth.

Eternally speaking, my baptism secures me from the eternally fatal. Any failure I encounter falls into the non-fatal category.

These non-fatal failures span the spectrum from forgetting to pay the invoice to running out of money and declaring bankruptcy. On one end we find a slight speed bump in the path and on the other end our lives are derailed for a season.

SACRAMENTAL ENTREPRENEURS AND THE THEOLOGY OF THE CROSS

Most baby sacramental entrepreneurs are not only new when it comes to starting ministries, but they are new when it comes to facing failures. Many are too young to have experienced it with any gusto, thus they stand with drool, unsure of how to make it through.

When a sacramental entrepreneur wades through the pains of failure, they are led to a deeper understanding of the cross. When everything falls apart, the sacramental entrepreneur clings to the only thing they've got left, the person and work of Jesus. In the moments where you are brought to your knees in the face of your own failure, the cross stops being just something you read about and becomes a part of your redemption story.

In Christian circles, we locate failure at the center of the Gospel: the message of the Gospel is one that hinges on the bloody, painful, suffering of Jesus for the sake of our failures.

One Pastor, Tullian Tchividjian, spoke of suffering when he wrote:

"Theologies of glory" are approaches to Christianity (and to life) that try in various ways to minimize difficult and painful things, or to move past them rather than looking them square in the face and accepting them. Theologies of glory acknowledge the cross, but view it primarily as a means to an end-an unpleasant but necessary step on the way to personal improvement, the transformation of human potential. As Luther puts it, the theologian of glory "does not know God hidden in suffering. Therefore he prefers works to suffering, glory to the cross, strength to weakness, wisdom to folly, and, in general, good to evil."

When I know the promises of my Savior, I can face any suffering that my failures might bring. I can face the truth about my condition. I can face the pain that comes with betrayal and loss. And I can face the hell that gets thrown my way.

Not because of my own strength, however, but because the One who fights for me lives in me.

"What then shall we say to these things?
If God is for us, who can be against us?"
Romans 8:31 ESV

Life's daily struggles are magnified in start ups. Especially when you leap into a new venture or new field, the struggles come out from hiding. When you desire a truly unheard of solution or edgy plan, a war will be waged against you.

"Lean into your suffering and lean into the cross."

Life consists of daily struggles. And often your drive for success shuts out the Gospel and runs away from suffering. Instead call it what it is. Lean into your suffering and lean into the cross. The pain refines the process and drives you to dependance.

FACTS

What do I not know?

Professionals, especially entrepreneurial types, have a problem saying, "I don't know." Even in the face of a question we don't have the answer to, we will hide our inability behind a veil of technical-sounding words so that no one will know we don't have an answer.

Routinely I encounter young entrepreneurial leaders whose egos lead them to believe they know everything necessary for their endeavor to succeed -- or believe they have to appear to know. Not only does their arrogance disallow them from receiving the very information critical to their project; it also alienates possible team members whose shoulders would help carry the burden across the finish line.

As sacramental entrepreneurs we aren't fooling anyone; we don't know everything. And we must learn to know what we don't know.

"How can I know what I don't know?" you ask. Difficult question, no doubt. I suggest you answer the question in terms of experience.

EXPERIENCE EQUALS KNOWLEDGE

I served in large churches and on multi-staff teams. I led ministry efforts in evangelism, youth, adult education and staff management, and never occupied the lead chair, for nine years before starting CrossPoint Community Church.

For nine years I learned what I did not know.

Many times we think we know something just because we read about it or watched a TED talk. My belief is if I have not experienced or accomplished the task, then I really do not know. I might know the facts of the matter, but transferring facts to execution is a skill set developed over time.

I can read about making a box with dovetails and floating lid, but until I have made a box with dovetails and floating lid, I do not know how to make one. And even once I have made one, I only know how to make one as an amateur. Amateur boxes are not pretty.

The sacramental life is an experiential life. Sacramental entrepreneurs value experience over class time. They strive for experience, submitting to a situation where they are not in charge in order to gain awareness and become more intimately acquainted with the process.

I lack knowledge and need to get it, preferably from someone who has experienced the road and arrived at the destination with some measure of success.

THE BRUTAL FACTS

Brutal evokes images of bunnies being devoured by wolves or my grandma executing a hen with her hatchet. I always thought there was a nicer, gentler way. She thought I was crazy and uninformed as to the ways of a farm. Headless hens resulting from swift, clean blows make for less pain and sooner supper. "To the jugular!"

The brutal truth often feels jugular intended.

Founders, entrepreneurs and bosses easily ignore the brutal truth because it speaks about them. Sacramental entrepreneurs need the brutal facts. Embrace the facts empirically, instead of emotionally. Allow them to drive your decisions but not to shape your identity.

Allow the brutal facts to become your friend, to speak to you about what you don't know.

HUMBLE PIE

Humility, then, is a key trait to a sacramental entrepreneur. Entrepreneurs don't say, "I don't know" without some sense of humility. Humility allows knowledge from outside yourself to flow into you and your creation. It stirs up a lifetime of learning and a daily embracing of "I don't know" so that daily "I am learning."

Sacramental entrepreneurs need experiential knowledge outside themselves. Humility places me under a teacher so that I can learn from her failures and leverage her knowledge.

When mixed with humility, an "I don't know" perception propels me to others who do know, who have experienced and perhaps, if their passion resonates with my passion, will join my cause. Entrepreneurs can easily fall into the "I need to be an expert" trap.

Experience, yes. Expert in one, maybe two areas, fantastic. But more than me being the expert, we need sacramental entrepreneurs to be learners. We need sacramental entrepreneurs who are willing to learn from people regardless of their creed, confession, or career.

We need sacramental entrepreneurs who know what they don't know so that they can gather people around the one thing they do know:

> *"And I, when I came to you, brothers, did not come proclaiming to you the testimony of God with lofty speech or wisdom. For I decided to know nothing among you except Jesus Christ and him crucified."*
> *1 Corinthians 2:1-2 (ESV)*

IF THIS STEP NEEDS SHARPENING...

1. Are you a wide-angled, big picture sacramental entrepreneur, or do you gravitate more to the fine details of life? What areas of your future start will be limited by your prominent perspective? How will it be enhanced?
2. List your top 5 fears. Ask someone close to you or a mentor how these fears will impact your efforts.
3. What knowledge do you lack? Be specific.
4. Ask your spouse or close friend to speak honestly about your top 3 blind spots. Then begin praying for those to be filled by individuals passionate for your cause.

STEP 3
PLAN YOUR STEPS

"An efficient plan will involve a flame thrower"
--Anders Brievik

"You would never start a restaurant with just one employee. You would at least hire a chef and a waitress. Maybe even a cashier. Why would you start a church with just a pastor?"

It was November, 1995 and I was sitting in the office of my senior pastor, Wray Offermann, in Decatur, Illinois, listening to a church planter from west Chicago explain his proposal for a new congregation. He began with the restaurant metaphor, and when he left a few hours later, I turned to Wray and said, "That's what I want to do."

Church planting had existed in my dreams since the early '80s. My wife, Julie, and I always thought we might one day become missionaries to Mexico. We loved the Hispanic culture and new adventures. Mexico seemed a perfect fit.

Following seminary, however, I served in large churches, on multi-staff teams, with a variety of gifted individuals. During that time I discovered I enjoyed working with a team of people rather than flying solo. I needed private, no-interruption blocks during the week, for sure. But I also enjoy building through team.

Since the only church planting models I knew parachuted the planter in, with little to no support, "missionary in Mexico" sat on the shelf. I knew enough of myself to know I wasn't fit for a solo project.

That cafe word-picture opened up another world to me.

Up to that point I knew I enjoyed starting ministries that connected lost people to Jesus, but my "start a new congregation" perspective was whacked. I thought solo-parachute was the only model available. I knew of no plan that incorporated what I was discovering about myself and how I lead.

Now, I had a plan.

No details yet, just a concept. But it was enough to get me moving in the right direction. Think team became my new perspective. "Create a team from the beginning" became my planning mantra. Everything else flowed from that.

I contacted the head of US Missions for my denomination, made an appointment, and drove to St. Louis. "What do I do with my desire?" I asked. "Tell a district mission executive," he said. "Everyone's looking for church planters."

Six months later, as I landed in Houston and hopped into the car of a couple leading a group of seven families who wanted to start a different kind of church in the suburb of Katy, I listened as they described the very type of church God had placed on my heart.

A few days later I gathered with local pastors, asking them the type of church needed in Katy. They responded like the startup group had the previous day. It was as if we were different siblings from the same mother.

Months later, when I returned to Katy this time having been formally called to lead this start, I remembered the importance of team. I knew we shared a common heart and a common desire. I now asked for a common commitment: "What type of financial commitment would they make to the mission?"

Money speaks to dedication unlike any other material good. It's why Jesus mentions it so often in the Bible and Cuba Gooding, Jr. immortalized it in Jerry Maguire.

"Money speaks to dedication unlike any other material good."

After leading them through a study of Luke 14 and how before the man built the tower, he counted the cost, I handed out slips of paper asking them to each tell me how much they committed to give over the next year to this ministry. I was committing at least 10% of whatever my salary would be. Would they join me?

Their response was enough to tell me their hearts were in. A month later my family and I arrived in Katy, ready to live out the passion God had poured in us. We were ready to turn our passion into a plan for the sake of our lost neighbors.

PERCOLATING THE PLAN

Our startup plan for CrossPoint culminated from years of gathering vision statements and dreaming "what if'" and reading the book of Acts ad nauseam. It came from exploring different ways to do ministry, playing a variety of pastoral roles, and then a year of focusing solely on Katy, Texas.

In a divine sort of way, we hodge-podged a plan together from torn pages of programs and magazines, ministries we admired, and the heritage and hearts of the launch team and our mentors.

And this didn't happen overnight.

Plans, like coffee, require percolating. It takes time for your plans to brew; give them the time they need. Don't rush your plans into existence before they are ready. Allow the plant to grow.

Abraham Lincoln said it well, "Give me six hours to chop down a tree and I will spend the first four sharpening the axe."

TELL ME...

A myriad of ideas exist concerning how to organize your plan. To help you think in terms of telling your plan, I like to think about startup plans in terms of six "tell me..." phrases.

- Tell me who and where
- Tell me why
- Tell me what
- Tell me the future
- Tell me how
- Tell me why, again

In my mind, one logically progresses from one to the next, beginning with the people in the community and the community itself, and moving from there to the "why." Then what you plan to do to bless the community. Then where you hope this startup goes. Then how you aim to get to that desired future, by when. Then finally, "Remind me once more why you want to do this?"

Startup lingo often throws around words like vision, mission and values. These words are commonly intermingled, confused, and used incorrectly, losing the value and clarity that comes with each one.

Values originate from those passions God placed in your soul. Values are what motivates your startup. Values flow from the heart and grab the hearts of others. Mission is second. It flows from values. Mission is "what you do" based on your values. Resources/strategies are "how you do the mission." And vision is "where you'll be once you've done it." Vision becomes the destination, a clear and compelling picture of the future you believe God desires.

Values, mission, and vision all share common ancestry, but they differ distinctly, each playing a unique role in the startup process.

TELL ME WHO & WHERE (PEOPLE & PLACE)

The plan begins with the people and community because they are the focus of your efforts. While your start should tie deeply into your heart, this new exercise class for young moms is for the young moms, not for you. Do you enjoy getting fit? Fantastic. Do young mothers occupy a spot on your admiration shelf? Great. A passion without a need is simply a hobby; when your passions align with the needs of a community, you have a mission.

Your goal is to become a community expert. Think like a missionary; learn the ins and outs of the community and those who call it home. Walk the streets and visit the mom and pop businesses. Attend worship on Sundays in the local churches. Set up appointments with those leaders who can open doors in the community: mayor, school superintendent, sheriff, city councilwoman. [2]

Think about your community. What are the top 5 things that your community loves? When you observe the behaviors of the residents, what values do you see? How important is family life? What about sports? What type of entertainment do people rely on?

As a sacramental entrepreneur, you should learn the passions of your community.

Is there one institution or activity that commands more control of the calendar than another? In the suburbs, the school district often owns the top spot. In some rural settings, the growing and harvest seasons set the clock. In vacation-oriented communities, the weather and recreation shapes the calendar. In cities and urban settings, ethnic rituals and traditions might drive the heart of the neighborhood.

Key questions to be asking:
- What is missing in the community that if present would bring a great blessing to the community?
- What resources exist in the community that could be used toward that need?
- What resources do you or your connections possess toward that need?
- What is the drive or transportation pattern?
- What roads see the highest number of people daily?

[2] MissionInsite.com is a great tool for learning about your community.

- Where and why do people regularly gather?
- What neighborhoods have the densest population?
- What are the living arrangements in those neighborhoods (single family, apartments, rentals...)?
- What do people do with their free time?
- What is the economic breakdown of the population?
- What is the ethnic breakdown of the population?
- What is the largest ethnic group and what are their values?
- Where do people shop?

TELL ME WHY (VALUES & PASSION)

What's your 'why'? What are the values that are embedded within you; the passions that shape why you do what you do.

Don't give me a list of ten values; stick to three, five at max. And at this point, don't worry about making your value statements sticky, that'll come later. For now, just help me understand why you believe God wants you to start this new venture.

For fodder, here are CrossPoint Community Church and FiveTwo's core values:

- Sacramental Faith (Jesus in me, in the sacraments, for the world; the church redeems culture, not becoming a sub-culture living its days apart from the world)
- Respect for All (A great, sincere love for all people, especially those of different color, economic bracket, education level, sexual orientation, family background; we help people belong before they believe, for belonging is the greatest sign of respect)
- Action-Oriented (Today is the day of salvation so we take action today so that more will get to know Jesus. What are you doing today to move the ball down the field?)

TELL ME WHAT
(MISSION)

You now have a better picture of the community and its residents. You also have a sense of the values and passions that are shaping the work you are starting in this community for the sake of people encountering Jesus.

What, then, will be the specific mission of this new work?

God gave Moses a mission in Exodus 3:10, "I am sending you to bring my people out of Egypt." A nice, simple, tightly-worded, action-oriented mission. "I am sending you" has a strong verb with a measurable outcome and "bring my people out of Egypt" implies participation on the part of Moses and identifies clearly the type of people Moses must focus on, God's people in Egypt.

The United States' Marine Corps mission grabs me, "To engage the enemy and destroy him." Like the previous one, nice, simple, tightly-worded, and action-oriented. "Engage the enemy" has a strong verb and gives Marines a measurable outcome, "destroy him."

Jesus gave the Church its mission, *"Go and make disciples of all nations, baptizing them in the name of the Father and of the Son and of the Holy Spirit, and teaching them to obey everything I have commanded you..."* Matthew 28:19–20 (NIV)

As a baptized Christian, the Church's mission is yours: make followers of Jesus from all ethnic groups by baptizing and teaching to obey. Sacramental entrepreneurs wrap this timeless mission in a language of the indigenous people in your community.

CrossPoint's initial ministry plan wrapped the Great Commission this way: *to build families who bring Jesus Christ to the world.*

As CrossPoint matured, we matured in our understanding of how Jesus is best experienced, namely, in the community of His people, the Church. I learn of Jesus solely in the Scriptures, but that knowledge is deepened in community with the body of Christ. We discovered that God had made us into a community church, one especially geared for those who did not know Jesus and moved to articulating the mission in a few new ways.

- For every individual who calls CrossPoint home, the mission is *"Bring my neighbor into my community of everyday followers of Jesus."*
- For individuals who serve or lead at a campus level, the mission is *"Be the community church for unchurched people."*
- At a worldwide level CrossPoint's mission is *"Catalyze sacramental community churches for unchurched people."*

The above missions stack one into the other, each bearing common marks and an identical common end-game (disciples) but with slightly different language and scope, crafted for the particular seat a person occupies.

As we've formed FiveTwo, we've rallied around our mission. *To fuel a movement of sacramental entrepreneurs who start a variety of sacramental communities that create baptized followers of Jesus from lost people.*

And the shortened version:
"We fuel sacramental entrepreneurs."

As you plan the sacramental community you will start, consider the people you want to reach and the end result you desire. How will their lives be different after encountering you and your group? Think in terms of life-change or transformation, not the initial product. The products and methods might change as the business matures, but the end-game should not.

If Starbuck's mission was to sell coffee, it would not dabble in teas and ready-to-eat lunches. But since it exists *to inspire and nurture the human spirit – one person, one cup and one neighborhood at a time*, scones, mugs, and indie music fit perfectly into their cup.

TELL ME THE FUTURE (VISION)

Vision is where you believe God wants you to go. It tells the story of your journey and describes your destination so you know when you have arrived.

The sacramental entrepreneur is like the airplane pilot inviting people to take a trip to Florida. If I have never been to Florida, you will need to describe Florida in such a way that compels me to want to get on the plane with you. You might state the vision in one sentence, "We are flying to Florida!"

Those who have been to Florida can somewhat envision the trip in their minds, but those who have not been to Florida have no idea what you are talking about. They need pictures of Disney World and swamp boat rides and year-round sunshine creating oranges and sun tans (it might be wise to skip the alligators and snakes).

Vision shouldn't require a ton of energy to grasp. Someone may not agree with your vision and they may not be interested in a trip to Florida, but they should be clear as to what it means to go on a trip to Florida.

Vision paints a future picture of where you believe God wants your startup to go. It includes enough detail that inspires others to buy a ticket and join you on the trip. This also explains why if you tell me we are flying to Florida, but somewhere along the way you change your mind and we end up in Kansas, I will raise a ruckus, want my money back, and tell the world you have no clue where you are going.

"Vision paints a future picture of where you believe God wants your startup to go."

Vision grabs the heart because it transports the heart into a preferred, divine future.

Contrary to what some believe, this part of your plan usually takes the more time to figure out. At least this was the case for me. I knew the values that drove me and the mission I was on long before I knew what the future might look like. This same order unfolded for CrossPoint and FiveTwo.

When crafting the vision, let the sediment settle to the bottom of the glass before you drink it. Write down ideas, create a poster to hang above your bed (your spouse will love you), turn the vision into a jpeg and make it the wallpaper on your computer desktop.

Let it sit.

What do you still like about it? What muddies the picture? Has the vision drifted away from your values? Has it gotten muddied by theological jargon that makes the destination unclear?

What picture has God given you for the future of your startup? This flows from conversations in your community and about your community. It flows from prayer and studying the Scripture. It flows out of being a missionary in your community learning and studying the culture.

FiveTwo's legacy vision (condensed): *An unstoppable force of 10,000 sacramental entrepreneurs who catalyze 1,000,000 sacramental communities for lost people by 2044.*

Vision should be clear, concise, and compelling. You might have a grandiose vision, and if this is the case be sure to have a clear pathway so that others can see how the vision can become reality.

"Vision should be clear, concise, and compelling."

FiveTwo's vision is certainly grandiose, having 10,000 sacramental entrepreneurs and 1,000,000 sacramental communities is a big goal, but we also strive to make the pathway to the dream clear. Plus we're giving ourselves a long runway.

Early in CrossPoint's infancy, one of our new leaders told me he had joined our ministry because while every start up church had a grand vision, we also had land and resources. He was able to see how the vision we had could become a reality.

Most people live in the moment, unable to see much farther than a few months, maybe a year or so. Visionary leaders tend to see farther and grander than others. Beware seeing so far and so grand that you end up going for a walk by yourself and beware of never seeing further than what is directly in front of you.

CrossPoint's vision (condensed): *A sacramental community church that helps lost people follow Jesus, generously blesses the community, creates worship locations for lost people in the greater Houston area and beyond, and equips sacramental leaders to create spiritual communities for lost people.*

TELL ME HOW (STRATEGIES)

A clear and compelling vision means nothing if you can't accomplish it. It doesn't matter how appealing the destination if you don't know how to get there.

When you pitch this plan to me and I ask, "How?", your answer should fall from the bag where values, mission, vision and needs have co-existed.

I would expect to hear the big buckets of:

- Marketing/Communications (outward-focused marketing & internally-focused communication)
- Community Awareness (in-the-flesh external focused activities)
- Community Building (in-the-flesh internally focused activities)
- People (the entire next step is devoted to this bucket)
- Funding (donations, grants, and fee-based)
- Operations (facilities, processes and managing the money)

I am looking for action steps, with dates or milestones attached. Dates on a calendar work well when the decision is event or task oriented. "Order the tables by October 14 because the grand opening is December 1 and we need to have them assembled in time." Milestones can help create incentive towards growth. For example, "When we hit 250 in worship, we will add a second service."

EXTERNAL

Initial strategies, for the first year or so, should tip scales externally more than internally. This cannot be stressed enough for startup churches. When I evaluate plans, I like to see how people will be cared for, for sure. Both must exist, yes. But in those early years, I want to see how new people will be engaged. In church plants, "caring for each other" quickly feeds our selfish needs, creates a clique, and becomes the entropy that stagnates growth.

Loving your community, living outside of your house or facility should consume the majority of your time in that early phase. When starting CrossPoint, we made 10,000 contacts in the community over nine months, serving and sharing in a variety of ways, telling them a new church was coming.

RESOURCES

Remember that the resources you need for this start exist in the community in the form of relationships. From people flow friendship, skills, knowledge, time and money. Build hearts and resources will follow.

A quick sidebar on funding, especially for church-workers... say "money" and sacramental entrepreneurs often shut down.

I suspect their personal stewardship beliefs are somewhat off. Maybe they falsely believe money and faith can be separated. I often find many sacramental entrepreneurs do not tithe back to the ministry they lead, yet expect others to. They end up unable to lead the people in the area of money because they are not practicing what they should be preaching.

Corporately, they fear offending and have not perfected the art of speaking money-truths with respect and logic. They default to melodramatic sensationalism that fails to find a home in the doubtful agnostic, or money consumes their personal life and they feel ill-equipped to speak on God's behalf in this critical area. [3]

And if managing money is not your forte, enlist a money-minded leader for your team. A wise money man once told me, "You can only spend a dollar once." God created a number of people gifted at managing money, stretching dollars to accomplish beyond the norm. Find that type of person for your leadership team.

TELL ME WHY
(AGAIN)

Wrap the plan with one more dose of "Why?"

Remind me of the passion that meets the need that brings the blessing that changes lives. Remind me of the calling that is much bigger than me, yet at the same time depends on people like me. Remind me of what Jesus is doing in His church. Remind me of people with the presence of Jesus in them.

[3] My friend, Chris Kopka, could be a great resource if this is an area you need help. www.brightpeakfinancial.com/team/chris-kopka/

IF THIS STEP NEEDS SHARPENING...

1. Have five of your leaders individually go through your plan. What makes sense to them? What areas sound weak or need clarification?
2. Are you aware of someone who has attempted to start a similar entity in a similar geography? If so, spend a couple hours with them answering, "If I were in your shoes today, I would…"
3. Personally, which stage of this step are you weakest in? Strongly consider getting training in that area. Nothing major or long-term, but you need to be confident in this step.

STEP 4
ENLIST THE PEOPLE

"First of all," he said, "if you can learn a simple trick, Scout,
you'll get along a lot better with all kinds of folks.
You never really understand a person until you consider
things from his point of view--until you climb into
his skin and walk around in it."
--Harper Lee, To Kill A Mockingbird

You have your passion, your perspective, your plan and now, people. You're going to need people to pull this off.

The sacramental entrepreneur who takes Harper Lee's words to heart lives to minister another day. He gains new people to the cause because he truly cares for them, regardless of their background, which allows them to discover camaraderie. Plus, by learning to understand the people they serve, the sacramental entrepreneur gains knowledge and wisdom.

If he will receive it.

The very strength of sacramental entrepreneurs, their passion, can become the startup's biggest weakness when not combined with a team of people. While passion drives them, passion unchecked also blinds them to potential fatal failures. The eternally optimistic, damn-the-torpedoes, I-want-it-today-so-let's-launch-tomorrow approach can lead to alienating the very people they hope to reach, leaving a wake of dead bodies, wasted money, and disillusioned followers.

People help the vision become a plan. People are the plan. They are the *why* and the *who* and integral to the *what.* Jesus' heart for people becomes the sacramental entrepreneur's heart. Our endgame is to enlarge His Kingdom.

If your startup will ever reach people, it must include people at every step.

Who are the people you need to include for the sake of your plan? Who are the people you are praying that God would provide? I encourage you to pray for leaders. Leaders bring more people. And when those people join your team, so, too, will their provisions.

Regardless of your product or proposal, here are the five types of people you should include.

A TEAM

Most entrepreneurs don't think team. They tend to be idea people who fly solo. The idea might originate with you, but executing and bringing your idea to life requires a team.

The brilliant animators at Pixar understood this well. It didn't matter how great the idea for *Toy Story* was if they couldn't actually produce a finished film. Having the team of business-men, storytellers, artists, and animators actually allowed them to make an idea into children's classic.

"If you give a good idea to a mediocre team, they'll screw it up.
But if you give a mediocre idea to a great team,
they'll make it work."
--Harvard Business Review on Pixar

Think of your team especially if you're planting a church. Most church planters have a diverse set of gifts which makes them great entrepreneurs, but this can also lead them to think that things are better if they do it themselves.

Build a team and don't let anything stop you. Teams bring knowledge you don't have, experience you lack, and wisdom that might be missing from your view. Even small projects benefit from having a team.

> *"Build a team and don't let anything stop you."*

Recruit leaders and help them find the right place on your team. Leaders expand the reach of the startup because they have followers or know how to find them. As you get to know these leaders, ensure that they also contribute strengths, abilities, and experience that is absent from your resume. This will allow them to play to the strengths that you cannot.

What 2-3 roles must you and you alone fill?

All other roles should be filled by competent leaders. Find other leaders that share your values and vision and find them the right seat on the bus. Help leaders define their roles so that they can serve effectively on their limited schedules, treat them the same as you treat paid staff in order to elevate their importance and value, and keep the team moving in the same direction.

If starting a church or ministry, pay attention to the faith of the leader you are recruiting, but do not let his spiritual maturity outweigh the skills or gifts he needs for his role. The worship leader needs a mature faith and the ability to articulate it, along with musical gifts and skill in gathering other musicians. The drummer may not need to know Jesus, but he does need to know how to play the drums. Many times over the years we have used second- or third-row ministry positions as opportunities to help people belong before they believe. Begin this practice early in the startup.

Our first worship band had a drummer like this. We found him via a music store flier, one of those tear-off slip deals that said, "Sunday morning gig. Need a drummer." He responded. We explained we were a startup church. He was actually excited about that, and he was a gifted drummer, exactly what the band needed.

A few months later, he failed to show up on a Sunday. After a number of phone calls, we discovered that he was in jail, arrested for speedballing, his girlfriend explained that this meant he had relapsed.

Were we wrong to recruit an almost-stranger in the worship band?

No.

Even though he left the ministry soon after getting out of jail, we were able to spend time sharing Jesus with him while he was here. We believe the Word of God never returns void. Everyone you run into is broken in some significant way. Beneath their smiles and happy families lurk struggles that sometimes pick the lock on the basement door and arrive with a jar.

I would add a non-Christian to my startup team if he met
this criteria:

- He was willing to dialogue about Jesus.
- He was willing to not speak against the faith we
  are encouraging.
- He was supportive of the cause driving us.
- He possessed the experience the team lacked.

I realize it may be hard to grasp a non-believer wanting to
help start a Christian endeavor, but many people find the
camaraderie attractive. Befriending them and loving them even
if they never believe allows them to experience the sacramental
presence of Jesus through you. It also offers your team the
outlook of the very people you are trying to reach.

When I look for team members, I look for direction rather than
destination. For a few key positions I want the individual to
have already arrived: she is an expert; he is a mature Christian.
The rest of the time, I am seeking a person facing the right
direction. I want someone who wants to learn and explore, but
he may not know the right answers or have the language down.
He is open to growing in faith and discipleship.

A COMMUNITY

A sacramental entrepreneur lives the presence of Christ,
believing that wherever he goes, there goes the Church. A great
sacramental startup connects that presence into the heart of
the local community.

Involve the community and its leaders early and often in shaping
the startup. While your team consists primarily of those who
have bought in and signed up, build a larger ownership by
enlisting people in the community in one-off opportunities.
Allow them to have a vested interest in your success by enlisting
them as consultants, experts and key holders.

"A great sacramental startup connects that presence into the heart of the local community."

Look for experts who live in the community. Partner with business, financial and church experts. Rather than seek to teach them, approach them as a student. Ask them to help solve your presenting problem. "If you were in my shoes, starting this _____, what would you do? Who would you make sure I talk to?"

God placed these leaders in the community as His instruments, sometimes ignorant to His work, other times well-aware and simply waiting to be invited. Buy them breakfast or lunch. Invite them to key meetings. Open the door to membership, but never make it a necessity of their contribution.

Help the leaders in your community discover the joy of giving. Help them be part of making an eternal difference.

A COACH

When I learned to swim, I was wise enough to know I could not do it without a coach. Since I was a stubborn, 53-year-old-man with an ingrained fear of water, I needed more than an instructor. I wanted someone who could match my stubbornness, yet bring a love for me succeeding. Someone who could balance compassion and truth, push and pull. Part trained counselor and part expert consultant.

I chose my daughter.

If you knew Abigail, you'd know she was the perfect choice. She is sweet but strong and a competitive swimmer who knows her stuff. She's experienced in working with children of all fear levels and has plenty of confidence to tell her old man, "Stop thinking that way."

Whenever we start a new direction in life, especially one we have not accomplished before, a coach is critical. He keeps your skills sharp, forces you to explore other ways of thinking, and pulls out of you what God has poured in you.

Seeking a coach implies you understand that you don't know everything. It requires a humble spirit, willing to adopt an attitude of learning, listening and following through. Sacramental entrepreneurs tend to ooze confidence; coaches help focus that confidence into the right avenues.

When choosing a coach, you can go one of two routes: someone with experience in your situation or someone with a clean slate. In some situations, you may want a coach that knows nothing about what you're working on . He may never have played the position but he knows how to maximize a potential leader's gifts . Other times you might steer toward someone who has effectively done what you are seeking to accomplish. She has been there, scored the goal and picked up the trophy. If possible, both should be from a sacramental background, sharing your faith values.

So start your search for a coach by asking yourself, 'How much experience do I want my coach to have? What kind of experience would be most helpful?'" Don't rush this choice. Take your time and make sure it is a good fit. Pay attention to chemistry; ask yourself, "Would I like to have a beer with this guy?" [4]

[4] If you need help finding a coach, check out CoachNet.org

A BOSS

Entrepreneurs enjoy being their own boss, accountable to no one. In the real world, 'no accountability' is a fantasy. Sacramental entrepreneurs at a minimum will demonstrate accountability to family and followers.

"If relationships form the basis for ministry, don't tell me you can't measure ministry."

From the moment you're on the clock, find a boss (an individual or a board) to be accountable to. Find someone that can hold you accountable for your character and your goals. Embrace being accountable for the sake of growing the kingdom.

This will likely mean that you should be accountable for measurable results, metrics that are ultimately about more people being in Jesus' kingdom. If relationships form the basis for ministry, don't tell me you can't measure ministry.

How many conversations did you have today?

How many people did you invite to join your team?

How healthy financially is the startup?

How many times did you pray with someone this week?

How many emails did you send out about the startup?

Non-profits often find it difficult to measure the soft side. A good boss will force you to go there and wrestle through what you will measure and why you measure what you measure for the sake of growing the kingdom. Entrepreneurialism is not for the faint of heart.

If your structure simply does not allow for a boss, then work with a group to define the goals you will be accountable to. Diversify between community industries, if appropriate, and publish them so all can see.

Hug accountability like your sweet aunt Sue who always brought you brownies.

A FRIEND

Starting new businesses and ministries open your heart to a world of hurt. Disappointment, depression, and moral temptations await the sacramental entrepreneur at every stage. Start praying before you land that God would provide a friend for the journey.

If married, confiding in your spouse seems natural. Startups tend to overwhelm the family, though, so a friend apart from family is a huge blessing to the family.

The tendency might be to look for a friend in the midst of the startup. While teammates should love being with each other, a friend outside of the mix allows you to be loved not for how you perform but for who you are. It also provides a door to life outside of the whirlwind, bringing much-needed diversion when stuff starts flying.

In talking with planter after planter this relationship is often missing. Sadly it was for me as well. We gravitate to those who have joined our cause, naively thinking they will remain forever. Some of us are fortunate, but others, not so much.

I share this need mainly from a desire to help you avoid what I experienced.

Suffering is divinely good for us. It shapes us; we are Good Friday people. Yet I can't help but think had I sought a friend outside of the plant, I could have avoided some of the emotional roller coasters so prevalent with planters. The ride might have been a tad less bumpy for my family.

I now have a number of these type of friends, all a product of many conversations over many years. We all share a common love for Jesus and His lost people, but we live in different cities, involved in different ministries, and mature enough to love each other without comparing pedigrees. Our friendship extends beyond our success or lack thereof; it's of the eternal kind and is crucial not only to my ministry, but to my family and my own well-being.

IF THIS STEP NEEDS SHARPENING...

My team members' names are
My community members' names are...
My coach's name is...
My boss's name is...
My friend's name is...

STEP 5
PRACTICE & PROGRESS

"Practice doesn't make perfect. It just makes you better."
--Tawa Suleman

For nine years I practiced starting a church without ever realizing it. God was sharpening me while I served as a pastor in the roles and responsibilities that I had been given. I started new youth servant events, new small groups that multiplied, new leadership structures, new worship services with personal testimonies and progressive music, new leadership development efforts, new ways to reach the community using technology... new became my middle name.

I was practicing and didn't know it.

PRACTICE BRINGS CONFIDENCE

A benefit of having practiced starting things for nine years was the confidence I gained during that time. I learned how to ask people to join a cause. I learned how communication keeps them engaged, especially during the time where progress is slow. I learned how organization allows more people to participate. I learned the power of fun and celebrating the little stuff because lots of little celebrations can offset a large disappointment.

During the startup of CrossPoint and FiveTwo, prior practice meant that often I had seen a similar situation before encountering again during my start. This gave me a sense of how to proceed. By no means had I ever started something as large as those two, but I had led a 20k plus dial-up phone campaign when we started a new worship service in Illinois, so I knew the basics of how to do it in Houston. I had started two small group ministries, seen the communal and discipling power inherent in them, so I appreciated the importance of that ministry and knew how to launch it well by involving as many people as quickly as possible. Prior experience helped develop the skills which led to confidence.

Confidence is magical. Just ask any golfer with a new putter he believes in or any golfer who always seems to hit the ball into the water on a particular hole. Confidence flows from skill but resides in the head. While fleeting, it cements into your psyche via practice.

If you find yourself starting up with little to no prior experience, then consider interning under a more seasoned sacramental entrepreneur for a few months. Bring a list of areas you need to grow in. Create your own development chart. Hire a coach.

When learning to swim, I practiced almost every day. Whenever I started new ministries for the first time, I found someone and somewhere to help me practice the ingredients necessary for success.

"If values don't result in behaviors, they're not your values."

This helped me gain confidence.

Whatever skills you see as critical to your startup should be practiced. If values don't result in behaviors, they're not your values. Practice the behaviors that reflect your values.

PRACTICE BRINGS PROGRESS

When I trained to hike up the Half Dome, I practiced by hiking up stadium steps with a weighted backpack. When we prepared for an 80-mile Boundary Waters trip, we spent Saturdays being schooled by an elderly female canoe expert who paddled circles around us because she used her core instead of her arms. When learning to swim so that I could pass the swim test, I practiced almost every day.

The swimming was often slow, but I took baby steps. I learned how to blow bubbles, how to kick properly, how to bend my arms and cup my hands, and even how to turn my core so that my reach was natural and fluid.

Each time my daughter pointed out the progress I made that day. "You swam that without choking!" Sounds silly when I write it, but those little steps helped me see how I could pass the test. I wasn't dead in the water. I was slowing moving toward the 75-yard finish line.

Progress creates momentum. It boosts morale, allowing us to see that the work of our hands is the right work to move us toward our goal. Recognizing progress in the early stages of a startup, especially in the slow, winding roads of finding funding or building the staff team, is an art. It's like learning to blow bubbles on the way to swimming 75 yards. By itself it doesn't sound like much, but stacked up with the rest, it results in an effective launch.

If the goal is to kick the ball in the net, to welcome a lost person into Jesus' Kingdom and teach him how to obey Jesus, then how are you moving the ball down the field? What steps are you taking to bring Jesus to him, and him, to Jesus?

SLOW & FAST & SLOW/FAST

Not every phase of the startup progresses at the same speed.

Some snail-paced stretches might entail months of study and info gathering. We spent four months flip flopping between worship at local churches and worshipping in our homes. Every other Sunday we would field trip to a Baptist or Assemblies of God or Methodist church to discover what expression God had planted through that community. We would then eat together, share thoughts of what made sense and what didn't, what we agreed with theologically and what did we not. These reconnaissance trips showed us what God was already doing in the community, helping us discern what unique expression He desired us to bring.

Other times the ride will feel more like a roller coaster, kind of like *the Master Blaster at Schlitterbahn*. You're in free fall, water's spraying you in the face and things are flying by you so fast you can't think. Once we started weekly launch team worship - about eight months post parachuting into Katy we were then in full-practice mode, with small groups and purposeful outreach events. We had just moved into a community recreation center holding 65 people. I often had to slow down my personal train, retreating for at least half a day a week to think and process.

During this season, we slowly saw God bring more people to our group. The progress was not so much in souls saved as in souls deepened, with the understanding we would be moving out very purposefully into the community in a big way once God brought the worship leader we needed.

In October of 1997 we found the worship leader, a great musical missionary named Joel Wetzstein. I love music but am unmusical. I make music sound better by not singing. In the early stage of CrossPoint, we had a boom box. I would choose music and play CDs on Sunday for us to sing along to; I was awesome on the cd. People were stoked that Joel took the position.

In hindsight, Joel's arrival was when we left the platform. We let the group know that during the next six months we would raise money for a larger setting and larger public launch. Joel had six months to recruit, train and disciple a worship band. We now saw beyond the little mountain peak we stood on, to the larger one beyond the valley. The milepost was planted.

From then on, the speed picked up. We had a date six months out; the game was on.

PRACTICE CLARIFYING

One of the most difficult challenges for the sacramental entrepreneur is to express, with clarity, his vision and passion. His thoughts race around his head like a cage of monkeys at feeding time, and not surprisingly, he can make sense of them. Every thought, every stream, flows into a beautiful ocean lapping at the nirvana of resorts…to him.

To his wife, his teammates, and strangers-about-to-become-best-friends, his explanations of the startup, his descriptions of next steps and hopeful outcomes are often punctuated with question marks instead of exclamation points.

Clarity brings unity while confusion dilutes commitment.

It's hard for me to join your cause when I'm not sure what the cause is or where I'll end up when we arrive.

Practice telling the story of your startup. Write it down so the words are succinct. Make each one count. Create a 30 second, 3 minute, and 30 minute version.

Start sharing with friends and leaders as soon as the idea sprouts. Ask them what makes sense. If they had to describe what you intended to do, how would they describe it? When they repeat it back to you, does their description sound like yours? What do you need to be more clear on?

One of my biggest joys happened with the launch of our third campus. While interviewing a worship leader, I sat in the back as the launch team asked the questions and shared the "why" behind this new location of CrossPoint. Hearing these men and women articulate our passion and mission sincerely, from their hearts, was worth the price of admission.

It was also a product of practice and training. The majority of them had participated in our Leadership Institute. They signed up voluntarily to help start this campus. Starting a new site 20 minutes from their home location was a natural outcome of their ministry.

When starting a ministry effort like another site or a stand-alone church, practice sharing your story by preaching wherever you can. I preached in congregations an hour away. I spoke at any gathering I could, in any state, always incorporating our startup journey.

Practice forced me to explain my passion and values.

PRACTICE GOING

A key discipline to practice as you start your new effort is community presence. You will be tempted to spend all your time crafting emails and phone calls and blog posts. All necessary, for sure, but sacramental entrepreneurs must lean towards relationships. Get out of the office and into the coffee shops.

Whenever possible, take someone with you. Model for people what you want to see in other leaders. Most people don't go naturally. You want to develop leaders who love the diversity in your community. Introduce them firsthand to the diversity. Schedule fun outings, with verbal reports due afterwards. "What did you love about that place? What was cool about that person?" Help them see God's imago dei presence in the people in the community. Help them wrestle with "What would it take for us to connect them to Jesus?"

When you practice going, you meet people in their settings. You enter into their world, smell their smells, and discover their unique contribution to the community. Learn to love them where they're at and thank them for what they do.

This practice forces you out of your comfort zone. It morphs you into a sacramental entrepreneur who becomes all things to all people that you might save some. It forces you to become "a servant to all, that [you] might win more of them." (1 Corinthians 9:19 ESV)

PRACTICE BEHAVIORS

Two value-behaviors necessary for any startup are hospitality and celebration.

Hospitality flows from a deep sense of respect for the people Jesus died for, all of them. It looks like no boundaries, including them in your events and activities with little to no prerequisite. It looks like lovingly entering into their worlds, bringing generosity to their homes with your love, your goods, and your time.

"Hospitality flows from a deep sense of respect for the people Jesus died for, all of them."

Hospitality is not just a "glad to see you" but a sincere hand-on-the-shoulder, "How are you?" followed by looking them in the eye and listening to their story. It will include giving up your seat for them, sharing your money with them, and listening with your heart to them.

Practice celebration every chance possible. It was dorky, but at one point we had a celebration practice called "Yay, God!" Whenever we had cause to celebrate, everyone would stand up, bend over with their hands between their feet, and slowly stand up to their hands waving over their head while yelling, "Yay, God!" Like I said, dorky, but everyone, including the kids, loved the goofy side of that celebration.

If you are a driven, type A, entrepreneurial type, you probably skip over celebrating. It might even appear a waste of time and money. Celebration builds a team and reinforces values and vision. It elevates individuals when you recognize their achievement and affirms their contribution to the mission.

PRACTICE MYSTERY

As sacramental entrepreneurs, our work is mysterious as well as material. Mystery includes prayer, faith conversations, sharing your vision one-on-one for how Jesus changes lives, asking God to use your meager words and actions to open hearts to His Spirit, caring for the people in your team and for those in the community. Mystery means Jesus is working in and through you in the community.

Our end game is more souls in heaven; the coffee shop or sports ministry or worship service we start is a means to that end. We need the means, but it should never be confused with the ends.

IF THIS STEP NEEDS SHARPENING, PRACTICE...

1. Starting new and small before new and large. Make a list of the small, new starts you have led. Can you describe the key learning in each situation? What one skill did you gain from each? Are you able to see the tools in your toolbox?

2. Recruiting individuals to your cause. Before asking the entire Chamber of Commerce, ask your real estate agent you bought your home from or the apartment manager in your complex. What is their opinion about your new start?

3. Describing your start. In writing, small groups, large groups. I preached wherever I could as both a recruiting tool but especially as a clarifying tool.

4. Explaining why. Why this startup here and now? What is God doing through you and your start that He's not already doing through other means in the community?

5. Starting from scratch. It's one thing to start from an existing group or entity. Have you ever parachuted in with only an idea?

6. Key behaviors. What feelings do you want to create in the people you desire to serve and reach? What behaviors in your staff and leaders will lead to those feelings? Have you trained your leaders in those behaviors?

STEP 6
CONTINUE TO PERSEVERE

"Success is stumbling from failure to failure
with no loss of enthusiasm."
--Winston Churchill

On Friday in August of 2000, the inaugural week of our preschool, our school director resigned. It was not pretty. I discovered the walkout when my secretary walked into my office and said, "Pastor, I think Betty is moving out of her office. She and her husband are carrying boxes out of the building." Joy.

Suffice it to say this was a potential coffin-nailer for a week-old preschool, in a facility yet to be dedicated, in a ministry only two years old.

Friday night I phoned every preschool teacher asking them to attend a meeting Saturday afternoon. On Saturday morning I gathered our Leadership Board and plotted out a strategy. Saturday afternoon we shared the strategy as a straw model with the teachers, modified it as a team, and appointed our Children's Ministry director as the interim preschool director. Monday morning I personally handed out a letter to every parent briefly explaining the situation and giving our detailed plan for moving forward. I also invited them to open house meetings on Tuesday and Thursday of that week.

God was gracious. No families left despite the change in plans.

Persist. Persevere. Don't give up. Let these words roll around in your head often in the startup process. There were many times I certainly needed to hear them. Startups provide a myriad of opportunities to quit.

Two times in particular call the sacramental entrepreneur to persist: when people leave and when plans change.

PEOPLE WILL LEAVE

Early in the startup of CrossPoint, I met with another planter who had hit the ground about 1 year before me, 30 miles south. As we talked the challenges of starting a church, he shared how in his experience, not all early-adopters stay for the long haul. Some moves occur naturally through job relocations. Other individuals will leave because they did not realize "she was going to have brown hair." When you are first recruiting and sharing your vision with people, those who buy-in 'see' the end game, but not with nearly as much detail as you. You eat, sleep and drink the mission. You picture the brown hair and brown eyes. They, on the other hand, love the skeleton you define for them, but they simply cannot take in all the details. In their picture, "she had blond hair."

That planter was right.

Not long after we were in the elementary school, two families left. One family I had walked with by discipling the husband and the other, part of the original group of 7, felt we should not take the risk of building a facility at this juncture. After much listening and discussing, they both decided to leave.

It was a blow not just to my ego, but to my heart. I thought our friendship could withstand the differences of opinion. I was sorely wrong.

You can call it miscommunication or detail overload, but no amount of describing the future will prepare people for a future different than what they envisioned. You should absolutely try to make sure their future aligns with yours, but understand you live immersed in it and they only visit on weekends.

Not everyone will love every bend in the road as you travel to the start of your new idea.

I'm not saying you should arrogantly ignore everyone. If no one agrees with your direction, you need to be prepared to go solo or think twice before packing up and going camping by yourself. You need strong leaders on your team, but also know that the stronger the leaders who have joined your cause, the louder and more forceful the dissenting voice will be.

When people disagree with direction, I try to evaluate their message in two crucial ways.

First I ask, "What core values drive this conflict?"

Heated conflict almost always flows from a disagreement in values. By discerning the core values behind the conflict, you can evaluate the importance of your direction based on values, both yours and theirs.

In the case of the two families mentioned earlier, the values conflicted over "acceptable risk," especially when it came to financial risk. The families lost trust in the leadership because the direction appeared foolish and too risky. They desired a slower, steady growth plan with no preschool needing a line of credit. Our "business model" approach, operating in the red until we reached a sustainable mass, did not mesh with their view of church.

Defining the issue in these terms allowed leadership to evaluate the level of risk we were suggesting and decide if the direction was the right one. The conflict served to unite us because we gathered around the core issue.

Second, I always ask, "Where is the truth in the criticism?"

Every criticism always possesses some hint of truth, especially when the critique includes your name. Entrepreneurial types tend to discount differences when sensing a personal attack. Dismiss those accusations at your own risk.

"'I can't worry about what people think about me,' is a fallacy."

"I can't worry about what people think about me," is a fallacy. It's easy to misdirect these kinds of criticisms, but sometimes your personality might cause offense. And when that is the case, you should take a careful look at the problem.

In the case of the financial risk, the couples were correct: I take risks and I should have clearly stated this indebtedness was a huge risk. What could I have learned in that instance? I learned, despite it taking years to sink in, that when the leader speaks brutal truth, it relieves others from having to do so. When sacramental entrepreneurs point out the abysses and address the 'bad news' head on, they are defining reality, a key leadership role.

I cannot lead you into a new future if we do not even know our present reality.

Early in the startup, especially in non-profit varieties, when individuals leave, dollars leave. This may sound crass, but the sacramental entrepreneur cares for both the individual and the entity. His responsibility is to bring his idea to life. He lives in the tension, believing that caring for the individual out of honor for Jesus is the will of God, while also believing that starting this new work is the calling of God.

Depending on your geography, the cause of people leaving might have more to do with relocations and job changes than with your leadership. That might make the pain of them leaving a tad easier, but there still exists a financial reality you must face.

Finances always play a role in organizations.

When those families left in the early season of our start, I hurt over the loss of friendships, and I hurt organizationally knowing the amount of offerings leaving our ministry. I prayed for God to replace them.

And He did, but not immediately, which necessitated changing plans and timeframes. Priorities had to be re-prioritized, staff roles had to shift slightly. Persisting was hard. Persisting through the times of relational loss requires a deep trust in Jesus to carry you through the hurt, realizing the loss is real but temporary.

Consider sharing the personal attack situations with your coach and allow him to help you discern the authenticity of the criticism in a way that matures you. At the end of the day, he might help you discern your gut and weigh the risk. He won't eliminate the hurt you feel when people you care about leave, however, because compassionate people always hurt when their friends leave.

PLANS WILL CHANGE

J.R.R. Tolkein, in The Hobbit, wrote, "It does not do to leave a live dragon out of your calculations, if you live near him." The problem for startups is that dragons don't always register their address. Some surprises can't be calculated in advance.

Plans will change for a variety of reasons, some because of you and others not. Your fallibility means your assumptions will be wrong especially in finances and people.

FINANCES

We built CrossPoint's original financial model based on $20/person in offerings per Sunday. Reaching the people we reached, with no church background and no innate reason to contribute financially, we assumed incorrectly: our average giving in the early years was between $15 and $17/person per Sunday. We also assumed we would have 60% enrollment in the preschool after year one. Our advance study, conducted by an outside firm, suggested that target a safe estimate. Reality was about 45%. Our assumptions were wrong.

I suspect we projected high because of my eternally optimistic outlook. My experience of how God provides in financial ways has often been miraculous in nature. Because of that personal history, I tend to assume He will somehow bring the finances we need.

By and large that has proven true, but not without timing differences. His generosity is boundless but my plan may not be His, which means how He provides might entail changes on my part.

Changing economies also entail changing the plan. GM did not consult you before closing the plant. United's CEO failed to phone for counsel before moving headquarters to Chicago. Loss of income in the local community may impact your business plan, forcing evaluation for sure and change, perhaps. Use this as a time to refocus and reevaluate. God is calling you to a new season where He has already prepared the way.

STAFF

In addition to false assumptions about finances, hiring staff revealed the challenges of bringing people onto a fast-moving train.

Before starting CrossPoint, I called a number of denominational leaders to ask them if they had ever attempted a large start, one involving multiple staff from the get-go. One story in particular I remember. This denomination tried a large start in California but after two years, it imploded. He credited the disintegration to the cost of doing facility and staff in California and their team was built too fast with a senior leader unable to corral the strong leaders into one direction.

When you build your initial leadership team of paid and unpaid staff, do your homework on past experience. Learn about behavioral interviewing. You desire individuals who have demonstrated the behaviors and skills; not individuals who want to do that. If they are not already demonstrating the values you desire, you do not have the luxury of changing their values.

This does not mean you wait to enlist people in any volunteer capacity until they are card-carrying members. Not at all, but the higher one goes in leading the effort, the less room they have for blazing their own trail. The more a person is entrusted with leadership, the more they are accountable to the agreed upon values, mission, and vision.

"When you build your initial leadership team of paid and unpaid staff, do your homework on past experience."

Be careful of falling into what Henry Cloud calls "defensive hope." "Defensive hope" is hope with no basis in reality or experience. Hiring someone who has not demonstrated the ability to start new efforts thinking that this time he will be able to; that would be defensive hope.

When building a team, look for past behaviors that demonstrate the values and skills your startup desires and needs. Evaluate the personal wake the individual left behind. Pay attention to team chemistry. I always ask the question, "Would I enjoy going on an eight hour train ride with this person?"

To some extent, staff who join a growing startup join a living organization who is growing from infant to teenager. What they thought they were joining can very rapidly change into their nemesis.

The bottom line here is that some of your hires will be bad ones. The party at fault matters only for learning purposes. Regardless of the guilty party, the issue must be addressed and moved through.

FOCUS ON THE HORIZON

In addition to my fear of heights and water, I get motion sickness riding in the back seat of a car. I know: wuss. I also know the trick to overcoming it: focus on the horizon. Pick a spot that doesn't move with the waves or the wheels. Look at it while ignoring all else.

The best spot for a sacramental entrepreneur's eyes?

The cross of Jesus.

The world's brokenness, your brokenness, were all redeemed on the cross. Whatever suffering and struggle you go through in your startup pales to the suffering Jesus endured. He endured and rose. There are no dead ends for Him, and this startup will not be a dead end for you. Nothing and no one are beyond His redemption.

IF THIS STEP NEEDS SHARPENING...

1. What is the most difficult situation — broken trust, failed relationship, bankruptcy, loss of parent or child — that you have endured? What lessons did you learn from that valley?
2. Are you too permissive with staff or too restrictive? What past or current employees could you consult?
3. Think about your family. Are they prepared for pushing through the difficult times of the startup? If married, will your spouse help push you through or pull you back?
4. Who do you have in your life that will pour courage into you? Have you shared with them how they play this role in your life?
5. Who on your team or in your life is wise when it comes to money? Ask them to teach you.
6. Who on your team or in your life is wise when it comes to hiring staff and choosing leaders? Ask them to teach you.

STEP 7
START PROPAGATION

"Therefore go and make disciples of all nations,
baptizing them in the name of the Father and of the Son
and of the Holy Spirit, and teaching them to obey
everything I have commanded you. And surely I am with
you always, to the very end of the age."
-- Jesus [Matthew 28:19–20 NIV]

The command is about everyone; it focuses on all ethnic groups. It does not stop with just one person becoming part of Jesus' family. It extends eternally, one with eternal consequences.

At the end of the day, you need to start.

Pull the trigger.

Take the plunge.

Stop writing and talking and start doing.

Set your landmarks and your date. Put something in stone.

Imagine what it will look like when your startup grows into the ministry you envision it to be. All of the time and sweat and energy that has gone into tilling the soil, planting the seed, watering, and weeding will be worth it. The seed that began in your heart and in your mind will grow into a tree bearing fruit.

If you want your startup to bear fruit, you not only have to prepare the soil, but you have to protect it. Protect people, protect culture, and protect systems. By protecting your startup, multiplication will happen.

PEOPLE

Jesus is the heart of the Church and at the center of Jesus' heart lies people. His love for us drove Him to the cross. His sacrifice for us redeems us for His purposes.

But not only us, the entire world. Especially that slice of the world serving alongside you in your startup and living alongside you in your community.

To protect them is to protect their hearts and their homes. Jesus does not build his Church apart from people. Protect the people He has brought to help you build His Church.

Protecting your leaders involves helping them protect their Sabbath. Startup mode tends to create drivers and runners. When your office is at home, it's easy to start working 24/7. As the leader, you set the tone for staff.

At a minimum don't invade the Sabbath of your staff.

Once a month my wife and I host a House Church for our pastors and their families. After worship we all join at our house for food, conversation, prayer, and if the weather is nice, swimming. We hire sitters so that the parents can rest and catch up with one another. Everyone brings a dish; we supply the meat and brew.

This simple gathering with no agenda has proven to be a force for great unity. We laugh together, hear what is weighing on each family, and talk with family and friends. We talk about anything but church. Church talk is off-limits. Sabbath for us starts after worship on Sunday.

Protecting your people also means you protect them from each other. No triangulation. "I ask that you take that to Betty. Have you spoken with her about it yet?" I will let the other person know so that reconciliation can be pursued, but I will not intervene at this stage.

"By protecting the people and staff who call the startup home, I am protecting the most valuable resources Jesus has entrusted to me."

When it appears an alligator is loose in the swamp and attacking one of my leaders, I am the first defender. I will not let someone destroy the character of another, especially someone on my team. I confront it head on, publicly if the attack has been public, so to protect the soul of that individual.

By protecting the people and staff who call the startup home, I am protecting the most valuable resources Jesus has entrusted to me.

CULTURE

By protecting your people, you set the tone for protecting your culture. Your people are your culture-bearers. They carry the values and heart of your movement in their words and behaviors. Knowing you love them enables them to more easily love your desires and direction. When they trust you desire their well-being, they will more likely do well for you.

Fortifying the culture takes a lot of energy in the early years of the startup. Over time the other team members and leaders will join you in self-policing. Initially, however, it is your primary job.

The task of safeguarding culture never ends. Entropy exists in every organization, including our churches. It is called sin. Left alone, the culture you formed in the startup season will denigrate as new people and new desires add into the mix. Constantly bringing grace into play, allowing the presence of Jesus to live in your group rather than be stifled, is the job of the leader.

Culture, as mentioned earlier, lives out in behaviors. Most people do not connect the two.

Consider developing a list of values with demonstrating behaviors. Help people see what you see, namely, that when I don't say thank you when a volunteer gives of their time, I am disrespecting her. When I hand someone a cup of coffee rather than make him pour it himself, I am honoring him. When I fail to give credit to another team member I am failing to serve her and allowing my ego to harm our relationship. When I sit with a community member in the ER while she waits for her son to be seen, I am demonstrating what the presence of Jesus looks like.

Beside behaviors, words shape culture. We might say words can't break us like sticks and stones, but we also realize the fallacy of that rhyme. Following a God who self-identifies as the Word, concern yourself with how words are used in your group. Are there particular words you believe are off-limits? Does your group know them? Which words especially bring joy to others? How are they regularly used?

Affirming, publicly, with words shapes culture. Words can be generous or draining. Public words of thankfulness and praise, for other members of the church family, flow into the air and seep into the hearts of those around. It sweetens the oxygen, leading people to take deep, rich breaths in your presence. Their souls enjoy breathing that air, enjoy feeling the invisible joy and warmth in your culture.

Two weeks before our preschool director resigned that first preschool year, my grandmother died. She had been my spiritual mentor, the single biggest reason I went into the pastoral ministry. Upon learning of her death, one of the couples in our ministry sent the prettiest, largest bouquets of flowers to my house. I'm not sure that I have seen as beautiful an arrangement ever.

My heart welcomed their generosity like a child welcomes chocolate milk. Even in my sadness there was light in my living room where the flowers sat.

That experience of joy especially in the presence of death is a culture issue I work hard to protect. We are resurrection people. Nothing could defeat Jesus, not even death itself. One of our group goals is for people to leave with more joy than they had when they arrived, especially if it was a worship service. Jesus will call us to deliver difficult, painful truth, no doubt. But His truth never negates His hope, which brings great joy.

Protect your culture. Keep the joy floating around the people so it floats into someone's heart.

SYSTEMS

A mentor early in ministry trained me in family systems theory. That season of learning and experiencing a holistic approach to helping families remains with me today, like an Amazon of books I can call up in a second's notice.

Your startup is one giant system, interconnected through people and process. The larger you become, the more critical the system process becomes. The more financially-based you are, the more critical the system process becomes.

Even small groups live in a systems environment. Your family operates like a mobile: remove one piece and the mobile seeks homeostasis. It always wants balance. Each time you add or subtract a piece from the mobile, the mobile shifts. The shift cannot be avoided. It has to be lived through. Everyone's world moves some.

When key pieces shift or change in your system, celebrate the shifts whenever possible. Understand that even so-called positive shifts involve pain. Call out the loss. Do not ignore it.

If you want your startup to be growing and multiplying, you need to pay attention to several key systems: care, communication, connection (both inside and outside the group), finances, and data. The first three deal directly with souls; the second two support the first three. All are important and connected.

What system will you use to ensure people you meet have an opportunity to become part of your movement time and time again? How will you get to know them? Will you keep track of who attends your events or frequents your store? How will you communicate with them when you do?

If able, recruit matchmakers in your startup to strengthen the relational web of your startup. These people know people and love introducing them to each other. They tend to remember names and stats and have an affinity for helping others find friends. They love to live relationally through the successful relationships of others. They are beautiful to watch in action.

One individual can typically care for no more than 10 people. Creating a 1:10 people system from the beginning allows you to provide the depth of spiritual relationship and mentoring people need and desire, while also scaling for growth.

A strong administrative/clerical staff person was part of our initial staff team at CrossPoint; when I started FiveTwo, that role was the first one I filled. More and more today, the accessibility of data and information not only necessitates managing it well; the expectation is it needs to be used well.

Remember to approach your launch date looking past launch day. Think about what's next: the next day, the next week, the next month, and the next year. Avoid focusing only on the bean sprouting. Where will it get its water and sun the day after that? That bean seed will produce many more bean seeds if protected.

"Remember to approach your launch date looking past launch day."

WHEN IS THE NEXT START?

An important flag to plant now is the date for the next start.

The effective startup envisions more startups flowing from it in the future. Not tomorrow, let the tree mature some. But at least set a date or a marker in the dirt naming when you will start the next one. Pin it to your wall, write it on a sticky note and stick it to your computer screen, or set an alert on your calendar.

It's time to start.

JOHN'S START

At the age of 50, John was approached to start a church in south Florida. He had served in a variety of established ministry settings, the most recent stint in a congregation whose ministry included the local university. He possessed both a love for the sacramental Jesus as well as a love for Jesus' lost people in his community. Over the years he discovered he was especially passionate about ministering to college-age students, the future leaders of the world. His leadership gifts, however, convinced him of the need to reach those students especially through other students.

John had another passion, deep discipleship. He had experienced the reality of walking with others as they together walked with Jesus. His heart desired to not only reach new people for Jesus but also to see God's Spirit mature these new followers for the long haul.

The sacramental entrepreneur in him desired to take his historical theology and wrap it in an expression that resonated with those outside the Church, especially college-age students and young families.

Not ironically, Jesus converged a number of these passions in this new call to south Florida: the area was a unique blend of retirees, young families and Florida Gulf Coast University, coupled with a group of donors who had both saved dollars for the start as well as committed to future funding.

Before John decided to take the call, he called me. We had been classmates in seminary and shared a love for seeing Jesus' Church grow without losing our sacramental heritage.

As we talked, it was obvious that John's perspective was a balance of "God's work done God's way never lacks for God's supply" coupled with appreciation for how much money was necessary to fund the startup with multiple staff and just how difficult it would be to lead people into the future. As the father of young family, with a wife whose parents were experiencing significant health issues, his family situation warranted serious consideration. The startup would be a whole family affair. He and his wife Lisa talked and prayed and prayed some more.

They decided to take the call.

John asked if I would coach him through the startup phase. I flew into Estero and spent three days with him, touring the area, meeting leaders, praying about the future church, beginning to pull from him what God had been pouring in.

One afternoon as we sat in a local bakery, John's passion for relationships and Jesus exploded out in a wonderful way: "... where relationships are everything" became both John's mantra and the future congregation's tag line.

Being a people person, out and about and meeting folks came naturally to John. Remember, he had been practicing this for decades, learning how to interact in ways that connected with others and affirmed their value. He visited with elected officials, the president of the university, local pastors. He joined the gym and met trainers. He spent time on campus meeting university students and at his children's school, getting to know the teachers on a first-name basis. He and Lisa bought a home in a newer subdivision, where everyone was new. They made friends with neighbors and had them over for dinner. The conversation naturally went to occupations and questions like, "Why Estero?"

Almost immediately upon landing in Estero, John also began building his team. The initial survey of the area showed an opportunity to create a ministry that blended ancient and future, retirees, young families and college students. The only way he saw that future becoming a reality was with a team that included someone gifted in reaching college students. After considering a number of individuals, some from the more traditional pastor track, God led him to Phil, an outgoing, deeply spiritual man whose passion for lost people was coupled with a desire to rewrite the rules on doing church. He had been searching for a place like Estero, with a permission and protection giving leader like John.

They were a perfect match, complimenting each others gifts and experiences. John gave Phil much freedom, and Phil gave John much respect.

Between my visit in March and Phil and his wife, Kyrie, arriving in August, John farmed the area, making relationships, determining future strategy, strengthening the donor group and identifying future leaders for the startup effort. Key to that process was a leadership team of elders, men whom he discipled so that they, in turn, could disciple others. These men helped steer the ministry, becoming a much-needed sounding for John.

Once Phil landed, leadership development efforts multiplied. Sometimes they worked alongside each other, other times they tackled individual areas. John brought the maturity and ability to speak into older individuals, but also a love for young and incredible joy for life in general. Thus he protected Phil while Phil built relationships and gathered student leaders for the new church. Phil and Kyrie began discipling individuals in small groups. Kyrie's job in social work took many hours, but her heart for young women brought great blessing into some key relationships during this phase. They also tried a number of social events at different times, practicing what worked so that it became ingrained in their calendar.

For the next semester, the team made more inroads into Florida Gulf Coast and developed its discipling philosophy. It also hosted a number of social/vision-casting events, seeking to build the group. Phil experienced the challenges of doing ministry in a transient college setting, as he sought to create missional communities that replicated. Perseverance was in order, and having a team to process with proved a huge encouragement.

In late winter, they decided to put a stake in the ground: the ministry would launch publicly in August using a space on Florida Gulf Coast University for worship. With six months to prepare for that, they continued their discipling groups but also began searching for a worship leader. After interviewing a number, they landed on Sam, a gifted musician who would relocate his insurance business into Estero, thus serving as a bi-vocational worship leader.

During the six months pre-launch, the team also developed their people systems for caring, communicating, and discipling. By giving themselves enough runway, they were able to progress purposefully without feeling like a gerbil on a wheel. This also allowed them to plan for after the launch before the Sunday to Sunday routine took hold.

They launched the third Sunday in August with over 200 people in worship, 80 of them college students. They are now off to the races.

IF THIS STEP NEEDS SHARPENING...

1. What behaviors cause anger to flare up in me? Are these flare ups valid values-issues or simply my narcissism at play? If tied back to the breaking of a core behavior, make a list of those behaviors. Lovingly share with your team what those behaviors communicate to you so that they can process that and then hopefully follow your lead.
2. Are there any mobile people-shifts I have ignored and need to speak about publicly with the team, to protect their hearts and avoid an explosion later?
3. Is there someone on my team I failed to protect that I need to go and repent to?
4. Who will I choose for my Care leader?
5. Who will I choose for my Communication leader?
6. Who will I choose for my Connection leader?
7. Who will I choose for my Financial leader?
8. Who will I choose for my Data leader?

let's start something new.

*Thanks for reading **Seven Steps to Start:***
A Sacramental Entrepreneur's Guide to Starting Strong.
For more information about the ministry of Bill Woolsey
and FiveTwo, check us out online.

fivetwo.com

AUTHOR BIO

Bill Woolsey's passion for reaching God's lost people has resulted in two unique ministries: CrossPoint Community Church (LCMS), a multi-site church with two campuses and two partner churches it is helping launch, with a vision for 20 campuses and partner churches by 2020; and FiveTwo, a "how-to" network for sacramental church leaders who want to more effectively reach God's lost people in the U.S. and around the world. FiveTwo desires to equip 10,000 sacramental entrepreneurs who launch 1,000,000 sacramental communities for lost people by 2044.

Bill and his wife Julie have been married since 1984 and have three children: Timothy, Abigail, and Samuel.

Made in the USA
Columbia, SC
08 August 2017